*I Wonder What Could Happen...*

# I Wonder What Could Happen...

Shannon Sharnel McLean

XULON PRESS

Xulon Press
2301 Lucien Way #415
Maitland, FL 32751
407.339.4217
www.xulonpress.com

© 2017 by Shannon Sharnel McLean

All rights reserved solely by the author. The author guarantees all contents are original and do not infringe upon the legal rights of any other person or work. No part of this book may be reproduced in any form without the permission of the author. The views expressed in this book are not necessarily those of the publisher.

Unless otherwise indicated, Scripture quotations taken from the New Century Version (NCV). Copyright © 2005 by Thomas Nelson, Inc. Used by permission. All rights reserved.

Printed in the United States of America.

Irina Bocharova as Graphic Designer/Contributor via Shutterstock for Front Cover.

ISBN: 9781545609224

In Loving Memory of,
## Rosalie McLean
12/30/1929-08/28/2015

# To My Beloved

**First and foremost,** I want to give all of the praises, honor, and glory to my Lord and Savior Jesus Christ. I thank him for being an anchor during my time of storm, and for keeping me throughout all of my trials and tribulations. I don't care what happens to my materialistic possessions, job, you name it! I know and accept that God is my provider and I wouldn't be where I am without his mercy and grace. Even when I walked away, he kept me free from all hurt, harm, and danger. Without him, I wouldn't be the woman that I am today and I am more than appreciative of all that he has done for me. Humility is a vital piece of who I am, and I am so grounded to love and accept everyone, even when it was hard to give that back to myself.

To my mom and Dad, I thank you for being a strong support system and showering me with the love and wisdom that you have over the years. Words alone cannot express the gratitude that I have for you and it is a blessing that I still have both of you in my lives. I never want to take you both for granted, and my only prayer is that God will bless us so that we can achieve our individual and collective dreams. Both of you have made so many sacrifices for me, and others. Your spirits are so giving and kind. I love you dearly.

To Lighthouse Ministries Praise & Worship Church, thank you so much for allowing me to share my gifts with all of you. Pastor Brenda and Sr. Pastor Gary are phenomenal leaders, and I thank you for giving me the platform to allow God's gift to be shared with your congregation. I would have never imagined even reciting my poetry in public at all, but it was nothing but God who called me to operate within this ministry. I love you, and God bless you!

Shirley Pearson, my maternal grandmother, I love you and I am praying that you can be the first person to hold a copy of my book one day soon. To my late paternal grandmother, Rosalie McLean: may you rest in heaven and be at peace. I look forward to meeting you again one day.

For those who I haven't named, I didn't mean to leave you out! I love and appreciate my friends and all of those who have stuck by my side. Shirley Davis, my godmother, has been such a kind and noble spirit in my life and I just thank you so much for all you did for me growing up! My nieces and nephews, aunts and uncles, etc. You all are dear to my heart as well.

I pray that as you journey throughout this book of poetry, God's spirit will speak to you and comfort you. I don't care what you look like, what it looks like, or any of the stuff that society gets caught up in. At the end of the day, we all need love and to feel accepted. Man looks at the outward appearance, but God looks at the heart (1st Samuel 16:7).

I humbly thank you for supporting me by taking out time to purchase a copy of my book, and my prayers are for God to move in whichever area of your life you need him to right now at this very moment. I am declaring peace, wisdom, and freedom from bondages, healings, and deliverance right now on your behalf, in Jesus's name, Amen!

Sincerely,

Shannon McLean

# A Message from the Author

*I Wonder What Could Happen* contains poems that I wrote as an adolescent all the way up until present day as an adult. These poems originally started right at my local church here in Baltimore, MD. One year the pastors at my church were celebrating their anniversary and I decided to present a poem to them that I had written. Ever since that day, I have been reciting my poetry in front of our church congregation.

As a young minority female growing up in Baltimore, writing became an outlet and expression for me. Crime swept the street corners, drug addiction affected many neighborhoods, and finding your place in society was an extreme challenge. Although I excelled academically, nothing pulled me the way that writing and music did. I've overcome many hardships, and God is the reason why I can present to you my dearest treasure: poetry.

However, it wasn't always easy. For many years, I internalized my pain, and it eventually converted into suppressed disappointment, despair, and depression. I wondered if God could hear my heart's cries, and I often found myself questioning his will and what my purpose was on Earth but I know now that the number one purpose is to serve him and worship him just for who he is!

Through my inner-most struggles, I gravitated towards God by hearing his word at church, and then regurgitating that same word through my poems. I realized that I had to be in control of my destiny, and not allow my past experiences to hinder me from growing into the woman that God wanted me to be. Since I have accepted him first in my life, I am honored to do his will and meditate on who he is in my life. I hope that I can speak directly to you because guess what? We are in this together!

My mother helped me come up with this title, and I am certainly giving her the credit that is due! The title of this book is a bit unorthodox as it concerns poetry, but I'm wondering what could happen if you open your heart to God, and receive his message through poetic form? That's the meaning behind it. My overall goal is for you to find comfort, peace, encouragement, and a deeper connection with our father in heaven. He's so awesome!

I am fulfilled to have stepped out on faith, and pursued my dream of writing my first book. Regardless of wherever you are right now in your life, just know that there is a God and he is one of love! We live in times of uncertainty, fear, and turmoil. I want to invite you, whether you are a believer or a non-believer, to see things from a different perspective.

One of the joys about embracing God is that his peace is surreal. He doesn't care about whether you are black or white, tall or short, etc. He is here to help you right now no matter how you are struggling or what areas you may be struggling in. When you accept him, all feelings of negativity and guilt fade. Forgive yourself, and step into God's realm of joy. It's an indescribable feeling!

You will find that the table of contents will be your guide to finding a poem that you may be drawn to based on the title or what you may be personally going through at this exact time. May your heart be filled with love, and may you be encouraged. Enjoy!

# Table of Contents

I. Dedication . . . . . . . . . . . . . . . . . . . . . . . . . . . . . vii
II. Introduction/A Message from the Author . . . . . . . . . . . . . . . ix
III. If You Need to be Encouraged . . . . . . . . . . . . . . . . . . . . 1
    a. Stepping into Your Future
    b. True Love
    c. New Blessings
    d. Why We Say Thank You
IV. If You Need to Connect with God . . . . . . . . . . . . . . . . . . 11
    a. Seeking the Kingdom of God
    b. The Power in the Living Word
    c. A Refilling
    d. You Choose
    e. Redeemer
V. If You Need to Be Comforted . . . . . . . . . . . . . . . . . . . . 31
    a. A Remembrance
    b. When I Call
VI. Final Remarks . . . . . . . . . . . . . . . . . . . . . . . . . . . . 43

# If You Need to Be Encouraged...

Encouragement is something that we often hear a lot about in church, but it's a phrase that I usually hear doing times of celebration or for motivational purposes. For example, I encourage my nieces and nephews to continue to do excellent in school. However, encouragement is something that we all need! Encouragement is especially needed when going through a rough time in life, and discouragement can often leave you feeling unsettled.

One of the things that I've learned in life is that encouragement doesn't always come as easily to you as you project it into the universe. Sometimes, it appears you must encourage yourself to keep pressing forward, never to give up, and to fight the good fight of faith!

But encouragement is something that I hardly struggled with growing up as a youth. I always pushed myself to do better and to strive for excellence, and eventually I knew that if God was leading me to do it…I had to **"teach"** myself how to encourage others along the way too. Even if it seems like the room is caving in on you, I trust and know that God has a specially-designed "door" for you to escape and enter into true peace. I encourage you to look up, and never down, or beside you.

Sometimes, we get discouraged when we feel unaccomplished in life or that the people around us or on social media has more than we do. You know what I say, my love? Don't worry about others and what they are doing! All of us are unique as individuals. That's how he designed it to be.

When we stay in our own lane, we can experience true peace. When I try to keep up with what everyone else is doing I get distracted. In this day and age, it's honestly easy to get wrapped up in the appearance and presentation of things. For example, we admire fancy cars, clothes, hair textures/styles, etc. But you know what? All of that does not grant one's happiness. Some of the richest and glamorized folks are miserable.

So, if you have been struggling to embrace yourself, your past struggles, and the fact that your image does not match up to others… remember to encourage yourself because God has a specific, and unique plan for you. I take joy in embracing my uniqueness. I don't want to be like everyone else! As a child of God, I am not supposed to be…

God has a unique purpose for us all, and his timing is not like our timing. A friend of yours may have married before you did, but that doesn't mean that God won't send you the right mate when it is time. You have to encourage yourself to look beyond who and what's around you. Look up! That's where your help and strength comes from.

Regardless of the state that you are in, there is a light at the end of the tunnel. Now, I'm encouraging you to open your mind and heart to unveiling who and what's at the end of that tunnel.

When you meet him for yourself, you'll learn what it is like to truly live and be set free…

Are you ready?

*If You Need To Be Encouraged...*

# Stepping into Your Future

There comes a time,
When you start a new,
God has opened a new door for you,
But it's your choice to walk into the new door,
With a head held high,
And confidence rests ashore,
That no matter what you choose to do or who you choose to be-
The blessings from our heavenly Father allows us to be competent,
And adequate to reach higher elevations,
But assumingly if you have faith,
Stepping into your future isn't a challenge,
It shouldn't be seen with fears or doubts,
But viewed through lenses which contain praises and smiles,
For there's no turning our backs now…
We can conquer it all,
There's no more looking back now,
And what we aspire to be,
Successfully we can be…
Successful you see?
Our faith and obedience can put us through,
Love,
Blessings,
Success,
Testing,
And many things that we shall take upon,
As the road paved to success,
Seems to unfold gradually,
But God will make away,
Funds to say,
That we can own a degree!
Doctors, Lawyers, Singers, and Writers;

*I Wonder What Could Happen...*

Cosmetology
Or anything we aspire to be,
And it's never too late,
Even when we make mistakes,
God will erase our past,
As new waves create deeper elevations to surpass,
The ones we used to have,
And now we stand today to continue paving the road to success,
To continue receiving blessings,
To continue being confidant,
And to continue being competent,
To finish this race,
That we've ran a few miles on…
Yet our time is still ticking,
We have greater works to do,
And with the help of you,
And you out there too!
You can help us to succeed,
And I will return the favor for you, indeed,
Because when the seed of God's foundation,
Has been stored within us,
We know that we can conquer all trials and tests,
We're striving to be the very best,
And if we hold onto this faith,
This belief,
God will work miraculously,
To pave the road,
A beautiful road…
As you step into your future.

*If You Need To Be Encouraged...*

## True Love

It is more than just a commandment,
To love thy neighbor,
It is more to understand,
From what is embedded on paper,
Because true love breeds within,
And will pour out,

God sent his only begotten son,
To portray the true meaning of love without a doubt!
We must learn to be,
What we seek,
Because God's love is unconditional,
Despite the habitual,
Trials and sins that we fell in.

And if he is love?
A definition that surpasses all,
Strengthening the weak and poor,
So, that they can be enlightened when their spiritual depth,
Needs to heighten,

Then what does it mean?

1st Corinthians 13:4,
Tells us love is more,
Than a word that we see,
It is a verb that should encompass every pronoun,
And being.

For the light that we have internally digested,
Will emit into the external realm of life,

*I Wonder What Could Happen...*

Without a suggestion...

For his love is sufficient,
And surpasses above all circumstances,
Which propels us forward.
When different things happen.

We are called,
Because of the blood,
That saved you and me,
To do all things through Christ who strengthens thee,
For it is his mercy and grace that we are covered by,

Which is why,
We must project what God has given us,
Onto others who are around us,
Because it can save a soul,
That is dying or lost,
It can pour the blood drops that were once shattered on the cross.

On someone who has never felt the feeling,
And experienced the everlasting power that love can yield,
For love conquers hate,
And protects us like a shield.

Because it endures forever and ever more,
True love is a witness for those who've never unlocked the door...

Here lies a command,
For all of us to take a stand in love,
Because the beauty inside of it,
Would never compare to the enchanting wings of a dove.

*If You Need To Be Encouraged...*

# New Blessings

Yesterday is gone,
A new day awaits you…

New blessings will manifest through,
And capture those who,

Are awaiting to seek God first…

Allowing your spirit man to thirst,
After his presence,

Is more reason to embrace the new year,
As God's "present."

It is encouragement,
For you to blossom into a flower that sprouted from cement.

There were times during the past days,
That your journey was hard and left you trapped in a maze…

But it is through those trials and tribulations,
That allowed you to defeat rising temptation.

And although it was not easy,
God helped you through,

By guiding your hand into,
A new door that awaits you.

And this year,
Is a gift to seek God more than you did before,

*I Wonder What Could Happen...*

Enlightening thyself with his word,
More and more!

Because this is the day,
That we rejoice,

This is the day that our inner spirit pushes us to lift every voice,
To sing unto the highest God who reigns!

I encourage you to trust God even when you have lost sync,
With who you want to be,

And if you shall stand in the wrong place,
Know that the battle is not over until he says it is!

God applauds you,
For being victorious no matter how hard it gets,

Because he was the one who pulled you through,
And now is the time to thank God for showing up during times of fear,

We serve a God who is here,
Allowing his word to pierce sharper than any two-inch spear.

So today we press forward,
In all our future endeavors,

We praise God for all of the stormy weather,
That yielded better days for me and you,

Because yesterday is gone…
And a new day awaits you.

*If You Need To Be Encouraged...*

# Why We Say Thank You

To the love that you give,
The mercy that is granted daily,
No matter the circumstances,

We say thank you.

To the broken hearted and poor,
The weak are stronger and the poor are richer than before,

And we say thank you…

For bringing us through,
Allowing us to see,
That everything's fine.

You'll let us see,
That new suns are warming us with better days to come,
No one could do it better than you do!

So again, we nod thank you.

For the countless blessings pouring out from heaven,
To the enormous works that you do,
All I can do is shout thank you!

Because there's no one like you,
Who can heal and deliver,
Wash away our sins from yesterday's mornings until supper,

There's no one like you,
Who will wipe the tears away effortlessly,

*I Wonder What Could Happen...*

Giving us new wisdom daily.

There's no one like you,
Who will love everyone,
Who will wrap your precious arms around all.

With you,
I am not judged because of my looks,
I am not judged because of my height

Or how I walk…
With you I am not judged because of where I've been,
But where I'm going,

And how I'm using you to guide me through everything
So again…
I say thank you.

# If You Need to Connect with God...

**Have you been** feeling lost? Needing guidance? All over the place? Maybe you are unsure as to where you stand with God, or how to begin developing an intimate and close relationship with him. I've been there before, and trust me the place that you are in right now is only temporary. However, I got out of that place by using writing as my form to convey my emotions and to speak openly to God about how I was feeling and all that was on my heart. Regardless of what you look like, God sees and knows everything that you are going through. I can't see the magnitude of the fight that you are facing, but you will come out victorious in the end as long as you continue to keep your eyes on Jesus.

The poems that you will read within this section are poems that I wrote to sociologically tie in how world events and my personal experiences has allowed me to connect with God. For example, when I think about those cold days that I walked to and from the bus stop as a teen, I know that it was God who kept me safe. The fact that you are alive and reading this shows that God is alive and he is real.

We often think about our problems, we beat ourselves up mentally for not being "good enough", and we don't feel as though God's presence can carry us throughout this journey in life. That's what makes it difficult to connect! We see our problems by distance, and we create a greater one between ourselves and God.

There will be hardships, trials, and tribulations. However, I connect with God daily to show him that I love him and appreciate him for what he has done for me, and will continue to do for me. I pray that this section will help you to connect with.God as well.

No one can love us the way that the Lord does. When I think back on the good and bad times, it fuels the fire for my praise and worship! When I think about the friends who left, jobs that didn't come through, accidents I avoided driving, and the fact that I'm still here? It further provides more than enough reasoning to connect with the one who has carried me and kept me. I am at this point in my life where I can't sit down on God. He's just that good to me!

However, I will admit that connecting with God can be challenging, in all honesty. But we can begin this journey together starting today. Enjoy!

*If You Need To Connect With God...*

## Seeking the Kingdom of God

He says, "Seek Me"
For my son was sent to give you a fulfilled life…

For even though your road might be weary,
Don't allow your eyes to get teary…

See, there's a passion,
In seeking God as you would do a hobby;
The more you practice
You aim better at obtaining stridence.

But there's a road out there,
That can cause you to stumble,
And as soon as you thought the ball was in your court,
You start to fumble…

For this journey has just begin,
Why is it of value to seek God first?
So that you can be enlightened,
Quenching your spirit's thirst.

See, you must hear me when I say this role is challenging,
One day you feel you are walking upright,
Next day the enemy is attacking with you every bite!
You might feel it's scary…

But don't you fear!

For the living word of God births truth,
And if you read John 3:16,
Where could you go wrong?
It's only right,

To seek the holy hands of our savior,
That were once clasped in intermittent prayer,

## I Wonder What Could Happen...

Asking "forgive them Father for they not know what they do",
So, what are our faults?

The overweighing burdens of me...
And you...
For I would rather seek his kingdom
Glory be to God!

But I don't want to stop yet...
We still haven't traveled far,
See, there's a will that will be done,
Through God's only begotten son,
He came to give.

So why is that on the news,
We see so many people dead?
Killing over a loaf of bread!

And God says, "I will supply all of your needs."
So why seek the kingdom?
It's not only for the blessings,

To your yesses,
Or the possibility of seeing Jesus in the light,
So, there's no more guessing...

But it's because,
We keep walking God's way,
And then we go our own on a different day...

So the cup is empty,
And he came to pour it with plenty,
To runneth over,

Pouring out blessings,
That we won't have room enough to receive.
For the sins of you and me,

*If You Need To Connect With God...*

Jesus paid for free!
There's no price tag,
That can be equivalent to our most holy one,

He is the only one who has wiped those tears,
Cured the addicted,
Addressed the convicted,
To set the afflicted free!

Now we see why the caged bird sings...

For the bars are just an illusion,
And the bird is free in its mind,
You can praise God,
Even when you doing jail time.

Because God is worthy,
He has all my praise,
God was the only one that brought us out on those cold, rainy days;
Bringing you sunshine,
Even when the forecast could not predict your pain.

For man cannot yield nowhere near what God can,
Because in this life,
We find that everyone you say is your friend is not your friend!

And as soon as you dipped into the waters of baptism,
You can see clearly now with 20/20 vision,
For you?
Jesus granted a life full of sin free living.

And we think it's hard being judged...
It's a cold world,
But readeth to your hearing for the almighty he,
Has called you out of this world!

## I Wonder What Could Happen...

So why is there a misconception,
As to who we represent as Christians?
We seek God even when it seems tough,
But doing it 1 out of the 7-day week just isn't enough!

For he came to see you smile,
Make it worth your while,
To stand strong,

You are mighty kings and queens!
Armored ready to fight,
For this spiritual battle,

Might leave a lot us baffled,
But it's never over until God says it is…
And when we leave this Earth,

We have a spiritual realm,
In the valleys where Jesus lives,

So I would rather seek him,
For he first loved me!

When people are dying,
Children are crying,
Thieves are lying,
And your spirit is weak,
So you fail at trying…

But God never stopped for you and me…
He hung his arms out,
Stretched out in pain,
So much agony!

And through the trials and tribulations that we testify,
We still await trial,
Which makes it more convincing,

*If You Need To Connect With God...*

To seek God's kingdom all of the time.

For man will attempt to pull you down in heavy weights,
Attempting to put everything on your plate,
But oh Saints!
There's so much joy,
In believing all 66 love letters,

That broke you from those chains,
Which once had you and I enslaved...
For the light within you,

Reflects out of you,
And just like a river flows,
Your spirit man will go,
To where the most high God shall lead.

Because he breathed you life,
And converted all of your wrongs,
Into one single right,
Which is to have everlasting life.

*I Wonder What Could Happen...*

# The Power in the Living Word

He says study to shew thyself approved,
For there will be challenges that arise amongst you,
With no clue on what to do…
For there is a work that will be done,
By seeking our holy one.

Although it is written,
You must embed it spiritually,
So that you won't have to battle mentally,
Or hurt others and yourself physically…
So I draw myself to God,

As I read Hebrews 10:23,
Knowing that the almighty he,
Will fulfill all promises as he keeps you and me,
Because his word fulfills life,
Bringing you out of strife.

For all the killing and sinning,
That the world has to be,
We have a God who is there,
Interceding for you and me.

There was a time we were all blind to the truth…

So now that we seek God,
Internal light reflects through,
And when we turn on the news,
We see so much brutality,
Wondering *will the world change its insanity?*

*If You Need To Connect With God...*

*Or will I even make it home safely?*

But God is in control!
So where the word leadeth me;
I will go.

Because the word promotes healing:

Shaking up deliverance,
Resetting this atmosphere,
Changing the global hemisphere,
Sharper than a two-inch sword,
So we grab onto a battle spear,

To fight!
For the word of God converts darkness,
Into light,
So I might feel better off without the ones,
Who don't understand me.

For those who walk upright,
Face persecution by humanity,
See, but Jesus called us away,
From the hands of the enemy,
What God brought you out of,
Creates a strong testimony!

Because the power of God is nothing but ability,
To wash away sins of the dying souls,
Those who are lost,
Confused on which way to go...

The word is limitless power,
And when we go to sleep,

*I Wonder What Could Happen...*

It seeps in hour after hour!
For there is nothing invisible,
As to what you struggle with,

And any sin you once encountered,
Jesus nailed it to the cross,

In a foreign language,
Like an Egyptian hieroglyph,

So, when people hate you for no reason...
The word of God will move,

Just as the four seasons,
Tell them that the power of the blood,

Is what saved me!
Jesus was the healer,

Molding my divinity,
Creating my humility,

Birthing an inner man spiritually,
So if you see me acting differently,

Or rather abnormally...
It's because the power of his blood,

Didn't happen accidentally!
But actually-

The spirit of the righteous,
Is enough to convince thee,

*If You Need To Connect With God...*

For God's love is what reigns,
And covers over you and me.

For he who raised his arms,
In turmoil and agony,

Died to see you and I live eternally,
The power of God is much more biblically,

An answer as to why you and I should rejoice happily!

For the power in his word,

Moves peacefully,
And rather effectually,

For there are homeless and those who are poor,
That have yet to experience the door,

To his riches and glory,
I seek God,

So, I can have the keys to unlock ,
What God will have before me,

And stored, see-
There is a God we can confide in,

When there is no one you can call "friend".
From morning to supper,

His word is food to the spirit man,
Which feasts on inner knowledge,

## I Wonder What Could Happen...

To guide you at ease.
For you?

Jesus came to provide internal peace,
So, you ask what is the definition of love?
For he who lives above,
Shows nothing but unconditional mercy!

For the power of God,
Will fill your spirit man,

When you feel empty,
And I would rather,

Stir up the power,
That the bible holds before us,

So that I can tell my spirit:
Don't give up!

Because the problems that you face,
Might make you desire to quit this race...

But the power of God,
Is what I will continuously abide in,

Because he blesses you and I,

With sufficient grace...
Just to keep living.

*If You Need To Connect With God...*

# A Refilling

Dear Lord,
Please give me plenty servings of what you are stirring up,
The fueling of my spirit could surely use a new cup,
Of that good ole' anointing and power,
Made fresh daily at the top of the hour!

And please don't forget to bless me with wisdom,
So that I can see clearer now,
With better vision,
Of who I am to be.

I guess in all my humor,
I'm seriously asking for a refill,
Not a small size,
But a jumbo sounds just about right!

Big enough to get me through another week
With a topping of Jesus's mercy, pretty please?
Because I'm desperately in need,
Of some refilling, indeed.

So, I heard you say that this would be for free?
Do you mean that I don't have to pay for anything?
All I have to do is be faithful and obedient?
And you'll refill my cup with all the necessary ingredients?
Wow, that's all I had to do?
Get on my knees and praise you,
And put my attention back towards you?

Worship you in all honesty, spirit, and in truth,
Walk boldly in my gifts as I keep my eye on you?

*I Wonder What Could Happen...*

That's something I should get use to,
Instead of making an excuse.

I'll pray and ask for you to guide me on what's next to do,
So that now when my spirit needs to be recharged,
I'll know where to head,
And it surely won't be Royal Farms!

So Lord I thank you,
For being who you are,
And for giving me a new fresh cup of anointing,
Without the need to travel far.

Because with you,
All I have to do is ask,
And before you know it,
My cup has plenty!

It will be running over,
With the overflowing of your grace,
And with this refill,
I'll be sure to be full for days!

*If You Need To Connect With God...*

# You Choose

True Christianity in its most beautiful form is transparency,
One's ability to walk in honesty and love,
Must never be hindered by what you assume is hidden,
From the good Lord above.

And true Christianity is about your lifestyle,
Your choices,
Learning how to master the art of ignoring the naysayer's voices,
If it doesn't align with the word of God…

Should it be voiced then?

Do we understand the meaning behind our "mhms" and "a-mens"?
Or do we just go along with what everyone is saying?

Because true Christianity is more of a walk,
Than it is a talk,
Our actions can either reflect lightness or dark,

But you must choose…

Just like I have to,
For the mistakes I've made,
I, too,
Have had to answer unto!

So what will you do?
When challenges rise against you,
And you find it's hard to pray and/or meditate,
Because in your mind,

*I Wonder What Could Happen...*

God's timing may have been a bit too late,
And what's done is done.

I can't think of just one,
But more than enough stories that relate to you and me,
And we've invested so much time,
Building our faith in ministry

But the bigger picture is larger than me and you!
Our features are different,
Yet our blood lines the same,
You praised him last week,

So what's changed?

It's a lifestyle...
You make the choice!
We can raise our hands and lift every voice,
As we rejoice,

And redefine what being a Christian means,
At core,
For the very fiber of your being,
Will soar!
Once you accept and decide...

So what will you choose?
How do you want to live?
Our spirits were meant to be alive, not dead!

So, reconsider...
Who it is that you want to be?
How you will choose to spend your eternity!

*If You Need To Connect With God...*

But first,
Remember that honesty is key,
We can't grow spiritually,
Without learning how to be,

Exactly who God called us to be!

So, what will you choose?

*I Wonder What Could Happen...*

# Redeemer

To be redeemed,
Means to be set free,
And when your battles form,
You have already been snatched from the hands of the enemy.

Because Isaiah 54:17,
Has told you and me:
"That no weapon formed shall prosper against thee",
Our spirits may have suffered for a season of enduring,
But joy always cometh in the morning!

So even while the sun seems to take forever to rise,
We fight these battles strong knowing Christ is by our side.

And what he was called to do,
Was to proclaim me and you,
As the ultimate living truth,
For there is no greater God than the one that we serve,

And he still protects us even when we do not deserve,
The mercy that is granted,
Along with our blessings,
Which is why we praise God,
Because he is our protectant.

When violence sweeps the nations,
Our redeemer lifts us higher to another elevation,
We are covered by his blood,
He who heals all infirmities,

## If You Need To Connect With God...

Calming your anxiety,
Rescuing you from insanity,
So we have changed our mentality,
To worship our most heavenly,
For his blessings will continue to pour,

Despite all that you've been through before
God has opened the door,
To live sin-free...
For he died for you and me!

With blood dripping down his body,
Scars and scrapes that were horrifyingly placed,
And he came to do this to save the entire- human-race...
And we worship the one,

Who has done,
All that he said he would do,
For his word will not return unto us void,
Neither for me or you!

We will sing unto the most high,
Who picked us up when we were feeling low,
Praying that nobody would know,
That sometimes we smiled even when it hurt us the most.

So unto God we praise,
For covering those arms over us,
Picking us up even when we could not raise ourselves up!
Because he has redeemed,
And set us free!

Just so that we can have another opportunity,
To see his face in eternity.

# If You Need to Be Comforted...

Are you going through the loss of a loved one, job, or facing a health issue? Regardless of your unique situation, your spirit may need comfort. The truth is that we all will face challenging moments in life where we need to feel comfort. One thing that I've learned is that the greatest comfort comes from our Lord and Savior, Jesus Christ. Man won't always be there to console you when you need him to be there; however, God will always be!

This short selection of poems will provide the comfort that you need. One of my favorites, "When I Call", was written after I faced a series of health complications because of an auto-immune disease. I was also in the process of managing my recovery after an unhealthy and toxic relationship that I was in. Throughout my struggles, I often felt alone and that God was completely "silent." God's silence caused me to become angry and to question everything. I placed my passion of writing to the side for three whole years as a result. Now, I've learned in my young age that time is so valuable and precious. I can never get those three years back, but I can certainly make the best of what I have right now.

If you are wondering if God is there, he is. He hears you and will uplift you right now…My struggle was that I thought that God was rejecting me. Yet, I was rejecting him. Sometimes, you won't always turn on the gospel station in your car, feel like reading scriptures, or even attending church services. Am I right? The truth about that is you will only cause time to wither away right before your very own eyes. Depression and the mental battles we face due to a crippled spirit can lead to a dark and lonely path in life. If you are feeling like you are there now, journey with me today so that you can grab hold of that comfort you need.

Remember that God does love you. Man will disappoint, reject, and even betray. Don't worry about what others think about you or say. What does God say about you? He loves you, and so do I.

*If You Need To Be Comforted...*

## A Remembrance

God's love always empowers any obstacle we face,
Any test we may have…

But God pulls us through the race,
And we always finish last,
As a winner.

Through crime filled scenes,
And violence that sweeps the nations…
As a people, we must find faith,
And peace,
By making a difference.

God's love always makes a better day,
Even though our yesterdays were rough,
And losing a job, family member, or friend might be tough,
But when we embrace what God has done for us,
We remember that there is no need to cry or fight!

Through the famines and poor,
That sweeps the nations,
As a people, we must find the Holy Spirit,
To guide us through making wise decisions.

God's love is forever present,
Even though we can't see or touch him,
He lives inside of us,
And we should remember-
That if we love him,
Then we should do the same to our friends and enemies.

*I Wonder What Could Happen...*

Through insecurities and low self-esteems,
That may have been an issue before,
Connecting the door with God opens positivity and confidence,
For when no one else seems to understand-
God is always on hand.

And...

He gave the greatest gift,
That one could ever have!
His only begotten son, Jesus Christ.

So tonight...
And for today,
Our tomorrows...

We as a people should share a remembrance,
Despite the situations,
That climb with elevations,
For issues that come upon us,

God is here,
And he will always be,
For you and me!

Through churches and congregations,
Where God's people unite,
We pray,
For our friends, health, and families,
We share the words of God,
To connect with him.

Again, and again,
As we praise him,

*If You Need To Be Comforted...*

We remember that his powers,
Are consistently working.

And making a difference in the world we live in.

So, let's continue to remember, embrace, and connect with our God,
Which is a remembrance for all.

Through the dilemmas we may face with our families,
And friends,
We must remember,
Why God sent them in our lives,
To begin a journey that we help each other...

God's love is linear,
Always flowing from one to another,
In a narrow direction,
Which manifests his grace and beauty,

Through the different people we come across,
We must remember that Jesus died on the cross,
To save all!
Despite race or character,

And if we as a people,
Remembers this,
Then how can we continue to put one down or hurt others we don't know?
We as Christians must love everyone,
Even when we assume it's hard to show.

So today let's not throw stones,
To ones we've never met,
Misjudge the ones that may be sent from God to help,
Us in different aspects to grow,

*I Wonder What Could Happen...*

We as a congregation,
Must not judge or frown our heads,
At those that we assume might be hungry, poor, or rich...
Because they could be God's angels sent,
In disguise to keep us in a positive direction.

Through the earthquakes and problems,
That may have been seen in Haiti and Chili,
We as a people,
Must continue to love each other!
Because anything can happen today, tonight, or tomorrow...
And although Haiti is a nation,
That was struck by a catastrophe,

God wants us to remember that he is here,
If he brought them through,
We must remember that God will do the same for us too.

But he wants us,
To stop taking the important things for granted.

By working as a union,
Supporting one another,
Helping one another,
And lending a helping hand to a struggling sister or brother.

If we remember these facts,
We as a nation,
And congregation,
Can rise above any fall!
And truly realize that God will save us all.

We can embrace this remembrance...
A remembrance for all.

*If You Need To Be Comforted...*

# When I Call

A part of me wants to call on you,
When I feel afraid, ashamed;
Rejected
And perhaps my spirit is dejected…

　　　　　I'm calling you…

So heavenly father do you hear my heart's cry?
Its beat stampedes over a rhythm of pain,
But some say these old Gospel hymns should take it all away…

But…
I'm still afraid of the unknown,
Who's next?
What's best?

*How am I even going to respond if the doctor's report confirms a positive test?*

But oh father you hear me!
I know that you do,
You said you would never leave me or forsake me,
But where are you?

Lord,
These pains and groans keep me up at night,
And people around me don't always act right,
So, who am I to be?
When I'm running on empty?

*I Wonder What Could Happen...*

How can I operate spiritually if I'm standing on nothing?
But who am I,
To question you...?
It's just I don't know who else or where else to turn to...

But heavenly father,
Do you hear my heart's cry?

Its sobs ricochet off my lullabies of pain,
Seas of tears spill out in vain,
And I just long to be anchored in you!

But,
I'm still calling on you,
So heavenly father do you hear me?
Is this road supposed to be this tough?
Or am I suffering for not doing enough?

Doing all that I can to feed my family,
Working grave shifts,
Just so that my kitchen table keeps food on it,
Oh Lord, do you hear?!
Why art thou silent when the test was supposedly over?

And I needed an answer yesterday,
For today and tomorrow's troubles,
Causes the fear of the unknown to leave my heart etched in sorrow.

I'm calling you,
But my dial tone shows a busy signal coming through,
Pain leaves my heart and nests in a river of blue,
Tears are steadily collecting on my pillows,
As I grudgingly wallow in sorrow...

*If You Need To Be Comforted...*

But one day I heard a voice,
Say unto me,
That just maybe,
I should switch up my routine?

Maybe I should search for you?
Instead of you trying to find me,
Maybe I'll pray and ask for what it is I need?
Maybe I'll shift the pronoun away from me?

And see who else out there,
Is in need.

So now when I call,
I'll know it was you who answered,
When I felt afraid, ashamed, and rejected
There's no denying that my spirit was indeed dejected!

You came in and wrapped me with comfort,
My heart smoothed over and was no longer made of stone,
But now of flesh...
Anxieties of the unknown became declarations of my spiritual independence,
And all of the gifts and blessings you gave me,
Guess what?
I'm walking in it!

So, who's next and what's best?
You Are! (And you will always be),
And if the sun doesn't physically shine tomorrow:

## *I Wonder What Could Happen...*
# *It spiritually rises within me!*

Even when the doctors speak illness,
I'll turn that thing around and speak wellness!
Maybe I should pray for those who don't receive me,
And ask for you to guide me into receiving them instead,

I'll leave this bed of anxieties and woes,
Casting out entities that you didn't instill within me,
Along with every infirmity,
While praying over my enemies!

Maybe I should appoint myself back to your grace and mercy,
Where you'll always abide,
And my spirit will instantly revive inside…

So heavenly father, do you hear my apologies and repentance?
Its volume triumphs over all humanity's existence,
As I widen my eyes,
To see the truth,
As I learn how to trust in you,
You'll answer.

Those pains and groans which once ached my side,
Do not compare to the beatings and sufferings you once sacrificed,
For me and all humanity!

And you commanded me and all of us to love our neighbors,
So people may not always act right,
But it's up to me to let my light shine bright!

Mhm,
Yep!
That's who we are to be!

*If You Need To Be Comforted...*

Strong and not weary,
Filled with love and not envy,
Speaking life and denouncing death,
Thanking you for a new day of breath!

Not just me,
But for you,
And you out there too!
For the word of God is for all those who sees, hears, and listens,
In spirit and in truth!
So,
I called you,
And you answered,
With a simple whisper:

    In that "I'll never leave you or forsake you", my child…

So next time I get weary,
Questioning myself and your whereabouts,
Excusing each scripture I once misquoted in doubt,
I'll turn back to you…

In revelation that the call was never intended for you,
Because it was meant for me to answer unto...

# Final Remarks

I just wanted to take out the time to sincerely thank you again for reading my poetry and sharing it amongst your loved ones, church family, and those who need inspiration. Spreading God's word through poetic form/spoken word is an amazing way to showcase the unique gifts that God blesses us with and how we can pull others into his arms by sharing them.

Each book that is purchased will have a percentage that will be donated to the ministry at my church. I want to bless and help those who've helped me which is why I am so grateful for your support. This book wasn't about me at all…It was about blessing those whose hearts needed to be open to a different way of hearing God's message. I am extremely grateful.

What's next for me? I am currently working on my second book which will be a 30-day devotional. I decided to switch (briefly) from poetry to a devotional genre in order to better connect with my audience. Boy, am I excited though! I am praying that if it be God's will, my second book can debut sometime in 2018.

In general, I would like to make writing a small sector of my career. There are other things that I would like to do in the writing/music arena, and I aim to dream big. With God, all things are possible. I don't place God in a box, and I encourage you not to as well! I want to use my gifts and talents to connect with others, inspire them, and provide more light into the dark world that we live in, you know? So much is going on in our society, and it truly is a blessing to just wake up and thank God for a new day. There are so many people from all walks of life who did not get the opportunity to see this day- so for that I am thankful to God, and I am thankful for your life as well.

My final words to you are to continue to be true to yourself. Live, laugh, and love. Life is too short to waste time bickering, complaining, and comparing. I thank God for who and what's in the right now- right now, ha-ha! Things won't always be perfect (that's a fact!), but stay positive. Whatever "Giant" you are facing right now in your life, look deep within yourself and unleash your inner "David." We are God's best creation, and we weren't designed to be defeated. Know that God wants the best for you, and that he truly loves you.

To my church family and Pastors, I truly love all of you from the bottom of my heart. For my family and friends, my love is indescribable.

Thank you so much again, and I am praying nothing but the absolute best on your behalf. I am sending prayers, good vibes, and energy your way at this very second.

P.S. Don't cry… Trust me, I am coming back. In the mean-time, stay connected. Feel free to e-mail me your thoughts about the book at shannon.s.mclean@gmail.com.

Greater works will be coming your way from yours truly soon.

XOXO,